Pieces
of Intelligence

The Existential Poetry
of Donald H. Rumsfeld

Compiled and Edited
by Hart Seely

Free Press

New York   London   Toronto   Sydney   Singapore

$f\mathbf{P}$

FREE PRESS
A Division of Simon & Schuster Inc.
1230 Avenue of the Americas
New York, NY 10020

FREE PRESS and colophon are
trademarks of Simon & Schuster, Inc.

For information about special discounts for bulk purchases,
please contact Simon & Schuster Special Sales:
1-800-456-6798 or business@simonandschuster.com

Manufactured in the United States of America

1   2   3   4   5   6   7   8   9   10

Library of Congress Cataloging-in-Publication Data Is Available

ISBN 0-7432-5597-6

Contents

Introduction

THE POETRY OF D. H. Rumsfeld (as he is known to the literary cognoscenti) demands to be read aloud. Like the epics of Homer, or modern African-American street poetry, Rumsfeld's oeuvre originated as oral improvisation, initially heard only by hard-bitten reporters and round-the-clock viewers of C-SPAN. Unlike most modern poets, who closet themselves with pen in hand, Rumsfeld surrenders to his poetic muse when confronting the boom microphones and iron-willed interrogators of the Washington press corps. During news briefings and media interviews, Rumsfeld quietly inserts haiku, sonnets, free verse, and flights of lyrical fancy into his responses, embedding the verses within the full transcripts of his sessions, which are published on the U.S. Defense Department's website.

A former Navy pilot, congressman, White House chief of staff, and pharmaceutical executive, not to mention a two-time secretary of defense, Rumsfeld has made a career out of turning divergent schools of thought into one coherent message. That versatility is reflected in his poetry.

At times, Rumsfeld composes in jazzy, lyrical riffs that pulsate with the rhythm of his childhood on the streets of Chicago. From there, he'll unfurl a Homeric tale cautioning us about the ways of bureaucracy. He'll fire off rounds of irony with a Western cowboy's sensibility, enough for some to call him "America's poet lariat." Or in poems like "The Unknown," his most disturbing work, Rumsfeld mixes Zen-like enlightenment and indifference, probably culled from his many trips to the Far East. "There are some things we do not know," the poet warns. "But there are also unknown unknowns."

For all its known and unknown unknowns, *Pieces of Intelligence* is less about national affairs than about the poet himself. From the era when gas stations held "little things" of glass to the leak-filled corridors of present-day Washington, Rumsfeld stands out as a man whose quest for real answers long ago required the kinds of questions no reporter dared to ask. "What in the world am I doing here?" he says, in "A Confession." His answer is no less a riddle. "It's a big surprise," and nothing more.

Sometimes comic, sometimes dark, D. H. Rumsfeld's poetry is irreverent but always relevant, occasionally structurally challenged and always structurally challenging. *Pieces of Intelligence* is the U.S. defense secretary's long-awaited first collection, combining precision-guided insights and a revolution in metaphorical affairs, to take the reader on a dazzling journey of the spoken verse.

I

War is Peace

The Zen Master Poet

The Unknown

As we know,
There are known knowns.
There are things we know we know.
We also know
There are known unknowns.
That is to say
We know there are some things
We do not know.
But there are also unknown unknowns,
The ones we don't know we don't know.

Feb. 12, 2002, Department of Defense news briefing

Needless to Say

Needless to say,
The president is correct.
Whatever it was he said.

Feb. 28, 2003, Department of Defense briefing

Muscles

Abu Zubaydah.
He had holes in him.
And he had some infections.
And he was not in great shape,
And he obviously talked
When people asked him questions.
And he said this, that and the other thing.
Has he started to give any intelligence?
I would assume so,
But anything useful?
It's not clear yet.
And I don't know that I want
To get into daily reports on it.
But his health is improving.
Now why don't the rest of you people
Go do pushups like this guy?
Look at those muscles!
He's got muscles in places
I don't even have places.
Look at him!

April 12, 2002, stakeout at the Pentagon

Polls

Opinion polls go up and down,
They spin like weather vanes.
They're interesting, I suppose.
I don't happen to look.

Sept 8, 2002, media stakeout following CBS's
Face the Nation

Political Lines, Invisible Lines

Deer and moose and elk
Walk back and forth.
People walk back and forth.
There are a lot of places
You don't even know
Where the border is.
That's the way it is.

Feb. 23, 2002, interview with editor of
The Sunday and Daily Telegraph

Chasing the Chicken

If you're chasing the chicken
Around the chicken yard
And you don't have him yet,
And the question is, how close are you?
The answer is, it's tough to characterize
Because there's lots of zigs and zags.

Nov. 14, 2001, with editorial board of
The New York Times

The End of the World

Puffs of dust
End up crawling
Up your leg
And hitting your knee
Because it's,
There might be
As much as an inch
Or two or three.

April 18, 2002, town hall meeting with troops
at Scott Air Force Base, Illinois

Changing

I don't find it hard to change,
But some people seem to,
And some countries seem to,
And some institutions seem to.
But it is particularly important.

Sept. 22, 2002, media availability en route to Poland

It

It's enormous.
It's not September 11th,
It's September 11th, cubed and squared.
I'd have to really go back
Mathematically
And see what cubed and squared
Would produce.
Do you know?

July 19, 2002, interview with The Washington Times

What It Will Take

The truth is, look:
If something is going to happen,
There has to be something
For it to happen with
That's interested in having it happen.

June 27, 2002, interview with The Washington Times

In the Red Sea

The Red Sea begins and ends.
And then there's an area
Just beyond the Red Sea,
And it may very well be
That people choose to do it
Before they get in the Red Sea
Or after they're in there—
Possibly, probably, certainly.

*Dec. 9, 2002, to reporters, en route to Eritrea
(speaking of smuggling terrorist cargo)*

Unanimity

Now,
Is here unanimity?
No.
Did anyone ever expect unanimity?
No.
Life isn't like that.

March 6, 2003, interview with CNBC

On Walking Towards a Wall

If you're walking towards a wall
And you decide you want to go to the opposite wall,
The sooner you make the correction,
The easier it is.
If you wait until you're right face up against the wall,
Then you've got to make a sharp turn.

June 24, 2002, interview with Bloomberg News

Doing the Capable

The United States isn't going to do anything
That it's not capable of doing.
And if we do something,
We'll be capable of doing it.

May 23, 2002, interview with Wolf Blitzer on CNN

Doing the Doable

What we are doing
Is that which is doable
In the way we're currently doing it.

Oct. 8, 2001, Department of Defense briefing

Secrets Revealed

Eighty-some odd percent
Of what is knowable inside the government,
What is known inside the government,
Is probably known outside the government
In one way or another.

Sept 8, 2002, interview on CBS's Face the Nation

Calibrations

You sound like my wife
When you say, "Briefly."
You're giving me calibrations.

*Feb. 14, 2003, response to question during Salute
to Freedom at Intrepid Sea-Air-Space Museum
in New York City*

End Zen

How does it end?
It ends,
That's all.

Feb. 8, 2003, media Q&A in Munich, Germany

II.

Three Haiku

In Command

A government is
Governing or it's not. And
If not, someone else is.

March 23, 2003, on NBC's Meet the Press

Evasion Haiku

I'm working my way
Over to figuring out
How I won't answer.

Dec. 3, 2002, Department of Defense news briefing

Impatience

It takes too long for
Anything to happen, as
Far as I'm concerned.

Nov. 12, 2002, Pentagon town hall meeting

III

East is East and West is West, but in Private Conversations, They're Really Behind Us.

Twelve Sonnets

Glass Box

You know, it's the old glass box at the—
At the gas station,
Where you're using those little things
Trying to pick up the prize,
An you can't find it. It's—

And it's all these arms are going down in there,
And so you keep dropping it
And picking it up again and moving it, but—

Some of you are probably
Too young to remember those—
Those glass boxes, but—

But they used to have them
At all the gas stations
When I was a kid.

Dec. 6, 2001, Department of Defense news briefing

Before Air Conditioning

I don't know how many times
I've been to Guantanamo Bay,
But it's a lot,
And it frequently was in the summer
When I was Navy pilot,
And that was back in the days before air-conditioning.

And it's just amazing,
But people do fine. I mean,
There are a lot of people in Cuba
With no air-conditioning.
I know that will come as a surprise!
But I was in Washington before there was air-
    conditioning

And the windows used to open!
It's amazing.

Jan. 22, 2002, Department of Defense news briefing

Happenings

You're going to be told lots of things.
You get told things every day
that don't happen.

It doesn't seem to bother people, they don't—
It's printed in the press.
The world thinks all these things happen.
They never happened.

Everyone's so eager to get the story
Before in fact the story's there
That the world is constantly being fed
Things that haven't happened.

All I can tell you is,
It hasn't happened.

It's going to happen.

Feb. 28, 2003, Department of Defense briefing

World View

One or two or three or four countries
Have stood up and opposed it,
And that is considered "the world" by people
For some unknown reason to me.
It's utter nonsense.
That's not the world.

Those are important countries.
Many of them are good friends of ours.
And they have a different opinion,
And that's fair enough. And God bless them.
They ought to say what they think,
And they ought to do what they think.

But they are not the world.
There are lots of countries in the world.

March 6, 2003, interview with CNBC

The Digital Revolution

Oh my goodness gracious,
What you can buy
off the Internet
In terms of overhead photography!

A trained ape can know an awful lot
Of what is going on in this world,
Just by punching
on his mouse
For a relatively modest cost!

As a matter of fact,
I'm trying to get
a picture of my ranch
And seeing what it looks like
From two-hundred miles up!

June 9, 2001, following European trip

Poindexter

I have met Poindexter.
I don't remember him much though.
I had known him
Years and years and years ago
When he was [in] a junior position
And he explained to me
What he was doing at DARPA
But it was a casual conversation.

I haven't been briefed on it.
I'm not knowledgeable about it.
Anyone who is concerned ought not be.
Anyone with any concern
Ought to be able to sleep well tonight.
Nothing terrible is going to happen.

Nov. 18, 2002, media availability en route to Chile

And Then It Leaks

Hundreds of things in this department
Start with an idea,
Here or here or here.
They then work their way around
With other countries—
If it involves other countries—
And then they start moving up a process...and then it
    leaks.

And everyone in the world thinks it's this,
And then it goes up another,
And it gets changed and fixed...and then it leaks
    again.

And it's different.
And then finally something gets decided,
And it's been fully vetted in the world
More than it probably needed...and then something
    happens.

Feb. 28, 2003, Department of Defense briefing

Reports

I don't even know who reads them,
But we're killing trees all over the globe.
And it's—they get put into the law
And then people just keep doing it.
If we just could knock off
Half of the reports
And cut the rest of them in half
And use a single color—
Like black and white—
And then put them
On the computer
And give them the electrons
And let them make the paper,
We could save so much time.

Nov. 12, 2002, Pentagon town hall meeting

The Economy of Oil

If a bad person owns the oil
And a good person owns the oil, different oil,
And the bad person doesn't want to sell it to you,
But the good person is willing to, it doesn't matter.
Because then the good person sells it to you.
You're not going to be buying this person's oil,
But this person's going to be selling it
To somebody else.
And the world price will be the same.
Everyone will have the oil they need.
They aren't going to horde it.
They're not going to keep it in the ground.
They need the money from the oil.
So it's not a problem.

*Feb. 25, 2003, interview with Al Jazeera, in response to
questions about a possible oil boycott*

Bad Only If They Ask

The Vice President has
Absolutely no economic interest
In any company
That he was ever connected with.
I have no economic interest.

None of the other people
Serving in the government
Have an economic interest
In any company
They were previously associated with.

Therefore, it ought not to look bad.
It only will look bad
If people raise the question
And say it looks bad.
It does not look bad.

July 15, 2002, interview with CNBC

Coward

Any businessman that went
To their board of directors and said,
"Well, board of directors,
"I think I'll build a plant in South Asia right now!"

The board of directors would say,
"Well, wait a minute, wait a minute!
"Aren't they?
"Don't they have forces
"On each other's borders?
"Don't they have a tense situation?
"Aren't they not talking?"

And investments don't get made.
Money's a coward.
People vote with their feet.

June 13, 2002, joint press conference with Pakistani foreign minister

Young at Heart

The minister and I
Were both elected
To our respective
Legislative bodies
In our early 30s.

And the minister and I
Were both named
Secretary of Defense,
Minister of Defense
In our early 40s.

And so,
For the younger people here,
I'm alerting you:
You could very well
See this gentleman
Back here in 2030.

*June 18, 2002, joint press conference with
Portuguese minister of defense*

IV

A Rose is a Rose, Unless the President Says Otherwise

Lyrical Poems

Transformation

Let me just say one last word
About this word "transformation."
It leaves an impression
That you start in an untransformed state,
And then you transform
And become a transformed state.
Life isn't like that.
Life is dynamic,
It's changing,
And really it's transforming.

March 6, 2003, Pentagon town hall meeting

Always Hard

It's always hard.
It's always hard.
Change is hard for people.
We know that.

You get up in the morning
And the first thing you want to do,
You don't want to change,
You want to do what you're doing.

May 20, 2002, interview with CNBC

Clarity

I think what you'll find,
I think what you'll find is,
Whatever it is we do substantively,
There will be near-perfect clarity
       As to what it is.

And it will be known,
And it will be known to the Congress,
And it will be known to you,
Probably before we decide it,
       But it will be known.

Feb. 28, 2003, Department of Defense briefing

Diggin' the Feeling

I like the feeling,
The idea of beginning,
And putting something in the ground!
Or in the air!
Or at sea!
And getting comfortable with it.
And using it!
And testing it!
And learning from that.
A lot of things
Just don't arrive
Fully developed, full-blown.
And there it is!

Dec. 17, 2002, Department of Defense news briefing

There's No Debate in the World

There's no debate in the world—
    As to whether they have those weapons.
There's no debate in the world—
    As to whether they're continuing to develop
    and acquire them.
There's no debate in the world—
    As to whether or not he's used them.
There's no debate in the world—
    As to whether or not he's consistently threaten-
    ing his neighbors with them.
We all know that.
A trained ape knows that.
All you have to do is read the newspaper.

*Sept. 13, 2002, media roundtable with BBC and the
Voice of America*

By Golly

Military people are organized,
They're capable,
And when the president says,
"Let's go do that!"
We say "Fine!"
I said, "Fine!"
I'm not stupid.
But I also said, "By golly."

*April 18, 2002, town hall meeting with troops
at Scott Air Force Base, Illinois*

So Many Things That Could Happen

You know...
Who knows what's going to happen in the U.N.?
Who knows what could happen on the ground?
There are so many different things that could happen.

You know...
As we're meeting, he could decide to leave the country.
It's a nice thought.
Someone could decide to help him leave the country.
Not a bad thought.
I just don't know.
There are so many things that could happen

Feb. 25, 2003, remarks to the Hoover Institution

Ode to the Facts

When people are working off the same set of facts,
They tend to come to quite similar conclusions.
When people are working,
Everyone is entitled to their own opinion,
But not their own facts.
And if you're all on the same sheet of music,
Why, you tend to sing the same song.

Sept. 24, 2002, news conference in Poland

Pieces of Intelligence

This isn't military business,
This is law enforcement business.
This is intelligence business.
It's gathering pieces of intelligence.
Scraps of intelligence.

This is what the FBI
And the CIA and sheriff's offices
And intelligence organizations
Around the world do,
And they live their lives doing that.

They gather this information.
They run down leads,
And they run down leads,
They hope.
And sometimes it works.

May 1, 2002, Department of Defense news briefing

Perfection

Nothing we have,
Nothing in the defense establishment,
Nothing you own in your homes
Is perfect.
Your cars aren't perfect.
Your bikes aren't perfect.
Our eyeglasses aren't perfect.
We live with that all the time.
Does that—
If you cannot do everything,
Does that mean you should not do anything?

Dec. 13, 2001, Department of Defense news briefing

A Classified Story

This has been an interesting subject for the press.
Everyone's had a big time with it.
And, the only time I've ever opined on the subject
Was when one day I said to the CIA,
"Gee, folks, why don't you give me an"
(I keep getting asked this question)
"Why don't you give me an unclassified piece of
    paper?"

And I brought it down here and I read it.
And for weeks afterward,
I was accused of having a different opinion
From the Central Intelligence Agency
Or for drawing connections,
Some sort of connection.

And this was repeated in the Senate,
And repeated in the House,
And repeated in the press.
And I really had a minimum of high regard
For the way the whole thing was handled.
So, I've decided
That I'm not going to go asking
For an unclassified piece of paper.

·   ·   ·

I don't need it.
You need it.
So what I do is
I read the classified.
I know what's going on.
And I'm perfectly happy.

Dec. 3, 2002, Department of Defense briefing, commenting on the department's reanalysis of intelligence concerning an Iraq–Al Qaeda connection

Lawyers

I just came out of a meeting with the president of
    this country.
And we talked about an access agreement
And some other arrangements.
And you won't believe it
But when I turned to our ambassador who's here—
Where are you Mr. Ambassador?
You're not here?
There he is.
He looked at me and said
It's waiting for a couple of lawyers
To come from Washington next week.
And I take him at his word.
So all I can say is,
He's a good ambassador
And he's pressing it hard
And I'm gonna go back to Washington
And press it from the other end.
And uh the only problem we've got is
We've got some lawyers in the middle
Who work like beavers
Who get in the middle of the river and dam it up.

*Dec. 12, 2002, in town hall meeting at Camp Lemonier,
Djibouti*

When

You're going to embarrass me
Because I can't remember
If it was yesterday
Or the day before.
I have certainly signed an order,
A deployment order,
With respect to the movement of forces.
And I just honestly do not remember when.

Sept. 20, 2001, Department of Defense briefing

V

Nine Poems on
the Media

Free Society

Oh, my goodness,
You can't imagine
The number of things
You see and hear
That are wrong.
It is just breathtaking
How much misinformation
Floats around.
I guess it's part of our free society.

Dec. 18, 2002, interview with Larry King, CNN

Not My Fault

The problem is
That people think
That news is something
That is announced
Before it happens,
As opposed to something
That is reported
When it does happen.
And I can't help that.

Feb. 28, 2003, Department of Defense briefing

The Pentagon

The Pentagon's a big place.
Hundreds and hundreds
Of thousands of military personnel,
Hundreds of thousands of civilian personnel.
Any reporter who wants to
Can go find one or more and—
That'll have a position on any issue,
All the way across the spectrum.

Then what they do is,
They write stories
That seem to fit what they feel
Might make a good story.
And they go around and ask questions
Until they find people that say those things,
And then they print.

.   .   .

Now I don't know.
I, they don't say who those people are.
So I can't go and say,
"Gee, have you got a better idea?"
Can't seem to do that.
Who they are no one knows.
It's a big mystery.
And life's like that.

July 29, 2002, media availability with Norwegian minister of defense

They Know Nothing

Anyone who knows anything isn't talking
And anyone with any sense isn't talking.
Therefore:
The people that are talking to the media,
By definition, people who don't know anything,
And people who don't have a hell of a lot of sense.

Sept. 22, 2002, media availability en route to Poland

This Rotten World

In this world of ours
If you get up in the morning
You're running a risk
Of having someone lie
And someone mischaracterize
What it is you're doing.

Oct. 7, 2001, briefing on "Enduring Freedom"

The Story

I was briefed on that story before I came down.
I have not gone over it.
It's interesting.
Let me try to put it in context,
And then I'll see if I can answer it.
I have no idea what it's about.

Dec. 17, 2002, Department of Defense news briefing

Not for Me

There have been a number of editorials.
I have seen one editorial
And one op-ed piece.
And on the other hand
I don't read them.

Nov. 18, 2002, media availability en route to Chile

Cheating Woman

She said she had a question
And she asked three.
I asked for an easy one
And she gave me a tough three.

April 26, 2002, meeting with troops in Kyrgyszstan

Template for Success

I think I probably said
To *The Washington Post*,
Although I don't recall precisely
What I said,
But I'm sure it's roughly
What I say all the time.

June 4, 2002, Department of Defense news briefing

VI

Because I Could Not Stop for Death, He Kindly Stopped for Saddam

Free Verse

The Barnyard

Where's the barnyard?
I see literally dozens and dozens
And dozens of pieces of intelligence every day.
And if you took all of those scraps
And looked at them,
The first conclusion you would reach
Is that they don't agree.
And therefore,
One can't know with precision
Until the chase around the yard is over.

Dec. 6, 2001, Department of Defense news briefing

Straight Talk

I mean, look,
There are no secrets around here.
This capability will be what it is,
And it will be fully understood by the world.
Other countries will know what we are capable of.
To the extent we have a capability.

Dec. 17, 2002, Department of Defense news briefing

Philosophical Journey

When you ask the question,
"Are you concerned?"
There's always a risk,
If one says they're not concerned,
That the headline will be
That the Pentagon is not concerned.
And it happened to me.
When I was asked
In a lengthy interview by BBC about the detainees
And how they were being treated,
And I described how they were being treated.
(They were being treated very, very well,
And properly, and humanely,
And consistent with the Geneva Convention.)
And we went through all this
And I described it.
And then he said something to the effect,
"Well, are you concerned
about how they're being treated?"
And I said something to the effect: "No."
   (Meaning, as I said, in the context,
   Because I know how they're being treated
   And they've been treated very, very properly
   And humanely)
   And that has roared around Europe

That the Secretary is not concerned
About how they're being treated,
When the context was that
I was not concerned,
(Because I know how they're being treated,
And they're being treated
And handled very, very well.)
Now, when you say,

"Are you concerned about these?"
And if I say, "No, I am not concerned,"
(About what as you cast the question,
Which is, "Are you concerned
"That they are going to be negative
"And take support away
"From the campaign of the war against terrorism?")
If I had answered and said,
"No, I'm not,
"Because I have confidence in the American people

"And in the people of the world
"Recognizing how much better off
"The people in Afghanistan are today
"Than they were!"
And yet I do have a concern.

Feb. 12, 2002, Department of Defense news briefing

Rules

Anything that I say
That I shouldn't have
Is off the record.
I want you to
Understand that
Right now, up front.

Jan. 12, 2002, interview with the Washington Post

Iraq

It's an enormous country.
You know, it's bigger than Texas,
Or as big, I guess.
I haven't looked lately,
But it is a very big place.

Dec. 23, 2002, Department of Defense news briefing

Not Well

We're not doing that well,
And of course, the reason is
It's not an even playing field.
We're a democracy
And they're a dictatorship.

So they control their ground,
And they manage the press,
And they lie repeatedly.
And we don't manage the press,
We don't lie—

No, we don't at all.

March 6, 2003, interview with CNBC

Ode to Cheney

It's this wonderful mix of a background,
Where he's steeped in the issues of government
And the issues of the private sector—
The political, the economic and the security issues,
Which is a wonderful blend for a human being to
    have.
Plus his heft as a person. And I don't mean his
    weight.

March 13, 2002, interview with U.S. News and World
Report

Central Question

It's awfully hard to know,
In fact, it's impossible to know,
Unless one just speculates.
I don't know how many people
Who live in an exceedingly repressive regime
  Actually like it.

Feb. 25, 2003, remarks to the Hoover Institution

Balloons and Music

You saw what happened in Afghanistan:
The people went out in the streets,
And they were joyous
And they had balloons
And they played music
And they welcomed the U.S.
Because everyone knows
The United States doesn't want to occupy Iraq.

Dec. 4, 2002, interview with Al Hayat LBC TV

Nothing to Do With That

Nonsense!
It just isn't!
There are certain things like that,
Myths that are floating around.
I'm glad you asked.
It has nothing to do with oil,
Literally nothing to do with oil!

*Nov. 14, 2002, interview with Steve Croft, Infinity CBS
Radio Connect*

What Should Be Spoken When
Saddam Speaks

He's an accomplished liar,
And every time he lies,
It's carried in televisions all across the globe,
And no one says that,
"This is a man who has repeatedly lied!
"And when you listen to him,
"You should be on notice:
"He's a liar!
"He doesn't tell the truth!
"He's got a history of denying
"And deceiving and tricking people!
"And so, listener,
"We're going to show it to you!
"But be on notice:
"It's probably not true!"
No one says that.

March 6, 2003, interview with CNBC

S.T.U.P.I.D.I.T.Y.

H.D.L.D.
It's high density—No.
High demand, low density.
In other words, we need lots of them
And we don't have many.
It's a euphemism for stupidity,
For not buying enough of what you need.
And so they've got an acronym.

Nov. 14, 2001, with editorial board of
The New York Times

Chicago

What's your definition of security?
I read yesterday,
I think there were something
Like six-hundred and sixty-six murders
In Chicago last year,
In a city,
Not a country.
Is that security?
Yes.
I lived in Chicago
And I think it's a great city.
I love it.

Dec. 17, 2002, Department of Defense news briefing

Behind the Curve

What happens in life is
In any one year
You can get by
Without making the necessary investments.
People do this in their own houses.
The roof leaks a little bit—
"Well, I'll fix it next year."
You do that for very many years
And you're behind the curve.

Dec. 12, 2002, in town hall meeting in Doha, Qatar

Freight Train

Every day I get up
And I go into a meeting
And someone starts telling me
About something that started
A year and a half ago,
Two years ago,
Three years ago.
A freight train got filled
And it's coming across the country,
And here it is right now,
And you get to look at it,
But you can't change it
Because it was loaded
Two and a half years ago.

April 18, 2002, town hall meeting with troops
at Scott Air Force Base, Illinois

From Mars

The fact of the matter—
The facts of the matter are there.
They're clear.
And I think that there's no question but
That if someone looked down from Mars
On the United States
For the last three days,
They would conclude that America
Is what's wrong with the world.
America is not what's wrong with the world.

Jan. 22, 2002, Department of Defense news briefing

Lovely Lady

I would like to interrupt.
Since you brought up General Myers,
Do you remember the day in here when General
    Myers said,
"Even my wife understands it?"

I'd like to introduce his wife.
Mary Jo, would you stand up?
There she is.
Look at that lovely lady.

June 26, 2002, Department of Defense news briefing

Observation of the System

It's hard enough just to keep track
Of the things that are really happening,
Without having to worry about
All the things that aren't really happening.

May 1, 2002, Department of Defense news briefing

Field of Schemes

Is the playing field this wide?
Or is it that wide?
One can't know that
Until one knows up above.

The president can't know that
Until he knows what the possibilities are
And what the risks are
If the playing field's this wide
As opposed to that wide.

Jan. 23, 2002, interview with Readers Digest

On a Day in May, Wishing for Fun

It would be much more fun for me,
If I could just go up to Congress and say,
"Golly, every single thing in there is just wonderful!
"I just think it's perfect!
"And we'll just keep getting more and more!"

And then you find you don't have enough to do it,
And then something has to stop,
And then somebody doesn't like it.
It would be much more fun.

May 20, 2002, interview with CNBC

Of Looters and Vases

The images you are seeing on television
You are seeing over, and over, and over,
And it's the same picture of some person
Walking out of some building with a vase.
And you see it twenty times,
And you think, "My goodness!
"Were there that many vases?
"Is it possible that there were that many vases
"In the whole country?"

April 11, 2003, Department of Defense news briefing

I'm Out of Here

I wish it were possible to do everything at once.
The procedures in this department
Start two years ago and then run,
And the freight train comes down the track
And it's filled way over there,
And until it runs to the end,
You can't see what's inside of it.
And every time you try to reach in,
It's like putting your hand in a gear box,
Because this depends on that,
And this depended on that,
And this depended on that,
And each piece depended on something else.
And you think you're making a wise decision
If you grab in the middle of it,
But in fact—

If all the layers that led to those things
Are not re-addressed back up,
You end up with a situation that is kind of ad hoc.
It's a perfectly responsible, isolated decision,
But if you make a series of them,
They end up random;
They don't end up with coherence.
And so all of this appetite to kill this,

Or do that, or start this,
My attitude is,
Look, we'll do it the best we can.
And as I look back, I say to myself,
"Not bad."

Oh, no, no. I love that ending.
If you think I'm going to mess that one up,
You're wrong!
No, sir!
I'm out of here.
I'm out of here!

May 1, 2002, Department of Defense news briefing

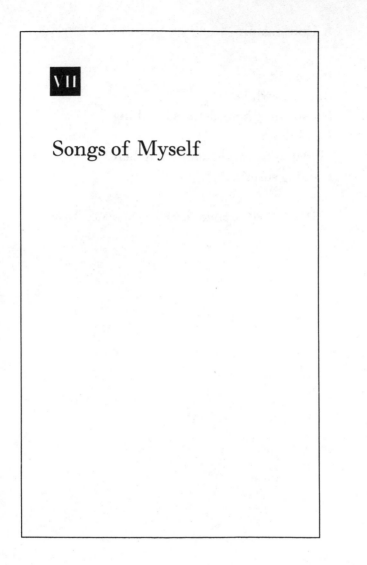

VII

Songs of Myself

A Confession

It's amazing.
Once in a while,
I'm standing here, doing something.
And I think,
"What in the world am I doing here?"
It's a big surprise.

May 16, 2001, interview with The New York Times

The Author

I will start by saying,
"I'm Don Rumsfeld,
"Dutifully saying
'I am Don Rumsfeld.'"
My affiliation is
the United States of America,
Ex of Chicago.

June 7, 2001, press conference after NATO meeting

Question Mark

I don't remember
That I've ever thought of anything
Original in my life.
I go around with people
Who are smarter than I am,
That know more than I do
And have done things I haven't done
And asked questions
And talked to them
And figure out what I think.

And when I figure out what I think,
I will then talk to other people about it.
And we end up on the phone
And I'll say what about this?
What about that?
What about this?
What about that?
And he'll have ideas
And we'll talk about things
And ultimately out of that interactive process
Comes what happened.

·   ·   ·

And trying to—
It's like trying to take a rubber band ball
And a string knot
And say how do you follow it through
As to where something came from.
I don't know where it came from.

Jan. 14, 2002. interview with Newsweek

Self-Portrait

I went to Washington
In Nineteen-fifty seven,
Working for a congressman,
Fresh out of the Navy.
I'm a broken-down ex-Navy pilot.
I hope you won't hold that against me.
All the planes I used to fly
Are in museums now.

Feb. 20, 2002, town hall meeting
at Nellis Air Force Base

Better In French

Explain this to me...
Just in English...
Oh, I was asking
If there was going to be a translation.
There's not?
Fair enough.
I'll have to do it particularly well then.
I always sound so much better in French.

June 6, 2002, press conference at NATO headquarters,
Brussels, Belgium

Meat

I now just got
The wrap-up signal.

Really I'm just
A piece of meat.

They just move me
From here to there.

June 7, 2002, with troops at Geilenkirchen, Germany

Gerbil

I feel like a gerbil.
I get on that thing
And I run like hell.

    May 17, 2002, interview with Armed Forces
    Radio and Television Service

Uh Oh

I can't remember.
I might have.
Hope I did.
If I didn't,
I should have.

Sept. 24, 2002, news conference in Poland

Rappin' 'Bout My 'Tude

I don't get—
I don't get furious.
No!
I get cool.
I get angry!
But not furious!
Yeah!
True.

April 10, 2002, interview with Marvin Kalb

People Who Meet People

It's helpful to me
To meet with people
Who are not people
That I normally meet.

Sept. 27, 2002, interview with ABC affiliate
WSB Channel 2, Atlanta

Them

They are terrific.
If you think of—
They really are.
And I don't say that
Just because I used to be one.

*March 6, 2003, Pentagon town hall meeting
(speaking of Navy reservists)*

I Love My Wife

I probably spend more time
With General Pete Pace
And General Dick Myers
And the chiefs of the services
And the combatant commanders
Than I do with my wife.

I'm on the phone with Tom Franks,
I would guess,
Two or three times a day.
I probably meet with him
Once every two weeks,
Including tomorrow.
Don't draw any conclusions from that.

*July 29, 2002, media availability with Norwegian
minister of defense*

Night at Camp David

We had our dinner, went to bed,
And I think he came in, and someone said,
"Do you want to go to a movie?"
I didn't want to go to a movie.
I'm not sure that was that night,
But it was one of those nights.
    In any event,
    That's the last thing I need, is a movie.
My whole life's a movie.

Jan. 9, 2002, interview with The Washington Post

Man and Wife, Talking at Dawn

My wife Joyce is here.
Every once in a while
In the morning
As I get up about five o'clock
And get ready to take a shower
And head for the office,
She says, "Don, where is he?"
I tell her that,
If I want to bring up
Osama bin Laden,
I'll wake her up
And bring it up myself.

*Feb. 20, 2002, town hall meeting
at Nellis Air Force Base*

The Proper Word

I ought to sit down and think about that a bit.
In fact, I think we all ought to,
If we want to serve our audiences well.
I haven't had time to do that.
What I do know is the standard words
Jangle in my head when I hear them,
And then I put them onto the subjects they're
    relating to,
And I know what's going.
And I think to myself,
"Gee, that isn't really as good a word
"as we ought to be able to find."
And I will invest a little time on that, and—
I'm still working on English though.

Sept. 20, 2001, Department of Defense briefing

BRACs

I am, I am,
On this subject, I am
As pure as driven snow.
I know the truth,
And truths, plural.
And there are several.
One is that,
For the most part,
People don't like BRACs.

*April 18, 2002, town hall meeting with troops at
Scott Air Force Base, Illinois (speaking of base
realignment and closures)*

Not Me

I had nothing to do with
Helping Saddam Hussein
And his regime against Iran.
We had, I think, one or two meetings.
The United States then
Did provide intelligence information,
As I understand it—
But I was back in private business at the time.

Dec. 11, 2002, in Qatar

Bad News Day

I'm not into the news business.
I'm into informing,
And developing,
Understanding,
Backgrounding,
And all of that.
I'm not into hard news.

June 27, 2002, interview with The Washington Times

Conceptic

When they told me what
This was about,
I sat down last night
And made some notes.
I'm not into this detail stuff.
I'm more concepty.

Jan. 9, 2002, interview with The Washington Post

Hello I Must Be Going

If you're in it for thirteen, fourteen,
Fifteen, sixteen months.
You just spend the first two months
Running around, saying hello to everybody,
The next couple of months making mistakes,
And the last few months saying goodbye.

*April 18, 2002, town hall meeting with troops
at Scott Air Force Base, Illinois*

Flying, Too

Now that is not always true.
Think of the B-fifty-two.
It's still flying just fine, thank you.
And so am I... thank you!

April 26, 2002, meeting with troops in Kyrgyszstan

My Era

You know what happened?
I met with a minister of defense from another
    country the other day,
And I am not going to tell you who it is
And you are not going to say who it is,
But during lunch one time he said -
(He was talking about something.)
He said, "You know that was in your era."
I looked at him, and he laughed
When he realized what he had said.
And I said, "You're right,
"But I kind of think this is my era too."

Feb. 2, 2001, en route to Munich, Germany

Me

I'm brusque.
I'm impatient.
It's genetic.
I can't help it.

Dec. 18, 2002, interview with Larry King, CNN

Final Poem

No, no.
    No, no.
        No, no.
            No, no.
                No, no.
                    No, no.

We really have to go.
We've run over 15 minutes,
I think.

Dec. 17, 2002, Department of Defense news briefing